Plantation Charm Wreath – How to make a wreath for your door

Plantation Charm

LEARN WREATH DESIGN

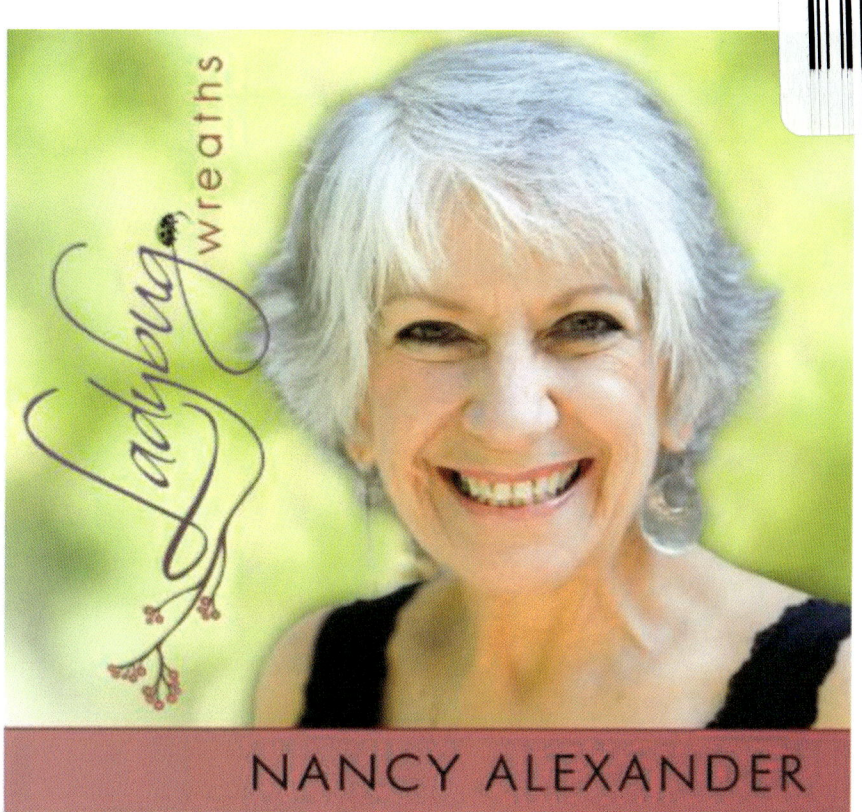

By World-Renowned

Floral Designer – Nancy Alexander

© 2014 www.LadybugWreaths.com, LadybugCertified.com pg. 1

Plantation Charm Wreath – How to make a wreath for your door

Want to Watch a Free Wreath Tip Video from Nancy?

Go To: **www.LadybugWreaths.com/sg**

Plantation Charm Wreath – How to make a wreath for your door

Publisher's Disclaimer

No part of this book may be duplicated, stored in an information retrieval system, or sent in any form or by any available resource, electronic, mechanical, photographic reproduction, recorded material, scanning, optically, either digital or analog or otherwise, except as permitted under Section 107 or 108 of the 1976 United States Copyright Act, without the prior written permission of the Publisher or Author.

Requests to the Author or Publisher for permission should be addressed to:
Ladybug Wreaths
203 Regent Road
Anderson, SC 29621

Limit of Liability/Disclaimer of Warranty: While the publisher and the author have used their best abilities in assembling this book, they make no representations or warranties with respect to the exactness or wholeness of the contents of this book and particularly reject any implied warranties of marketability or appropriateness for a particular purpose. No warranty may be developed or continued by sales representatives or written sales materials.

The information and methods contained herein may not be useful for your circumstances. The reader should confer with a professional where suitable. Neither the publisher nor the author shall be responsible for any loss of profit or any other commercial injuries, including but not limited to special, incidental, significant, or other damages.

If you would like to begin receiving our popular and Free newsletter with valuable information, visit: http://www.LadybugWreaths.com. We would love to add you to our subscriber list.

Please email nancy@LadybugWreaths.com to report illegal distribution.

As of the writing of this book, all information is current. Please note that over time, this type of information may change – especially when writing and picturing seasonal items.

Plantation Charm Wreath – How to make a wreath for your door

CONTENTS

ABOUT THE AUTHOR 7

INTRODUCTION 10

ITEMS YOU WILL NEED 12

MAKING YOUR WREATH 13

    CHAPTER 1 – LET'S MAKE A WREATH 13

    Chapter 2 – WILD HONEYSUCKLE 14

    CHAPTER 3 – INSERTING WILD HONEYSUCKLE 17

    CHAPTER 4 – HOW TO USE A FLORAL PICK 25

    CHAPTER 5 – USING FLORAL TAPE 28

    CHAPTER 6 – LET'S ADD LUCIOUS FRUIT 29

    CHAPTER 7 – MAGNIFICENT MAGNOLIAS 41

    CHAPTER 8 – MUST HAVE REAL - LOOKING LEMONS 44

    CHAPTER 9 –GREENS MAKES such A DIFFERENCE 52

    CHAPTER 10 – GOTTA HAVE A SWEET BIRD NEST 69

    CHAPTER 11 – FINAL TOUCHES 74

    CHAPTER 12 – A DOUBLE BOW IS EASY 94

    CHAPTER 13 – EXTRA GRASSES, GREENERY, AND TWIGS 115

    CHAPTER 14 – FINISHED WREATH 139

Appendix – RESOURCE PAGE 140

appendix – GETTING STARTED MAKING WREATHS 143

Appendix – How to Decorate a Wreath 150

Appendix – How to Sell Your Wreaths 157

© 2014 www.LadybugWreaths.com, LadybugCertified.com

ABOUT THE AUTHOR

Nancy Alexander is a wife, mother, Mimi, sister, best friend, and child of God.

As a Dreamer, Artisan, Teacher, Public Speaker, Coach and Internet Entrepreneur, it didn't take long for her to become known as a world-renowned Floral and Interior Designer.

After over 30 years of running her own businesses, she now sells popular floral designs, as well as her how-to, instructional DVDs and downloadable videos.

But, that's not all! Nancy is a published author offering several popular Books. Her life story is being written with a published author.

Nancy is blessed to know, work, and partner with many of the most talented "Internet Entrepreneurs" in the business.

Nancy **LOVES** her students, as she shares in their joy and excitement with every accomplishment!

 "**Nancy's dreams are to make YOUR dreams come true by equipping and teaching YOU to become a success!**" You'll quite often hear Nancy's encouraging words saying "You Can Do It!...I Know YOU Can!"

In the last 10 years well over 3,000 wreaths have been shipped to happy customers all over the world. She has sold thousands of videos and e-books which teach her customers how to design and sell their own floral creations!

Nancy, and her best friend and partner, Linda Joseph, offer private and group coaching. This one-on-one or group coaching has made a huge difference in many lives. You can find more information about these coaching venues on their latest website: **www.PassionIntoProfits.com**

Their coaching/membership site, **www.BestOfNancy.com** encourages and trains women to develop their "artisan" skills as they learn to sell and promote crafts and products online through many venues.

Another Ladybug Wreath's site, **www.LadybugCertified.com** provides the exact same supplies Nancy uses in all her wreaths. Available from Amazon, shipping is FREE with Amazon Prime. Benefits are…no Sales Tax ID is required; no case quantities; no minimums; and super-fast shipping.

Group & Private (VIP) workshops offered in her home studio are such fun. After experiencing a "Studio Day" with Nancy, each lady departs with a gorgeous wreath and an easel. They possess the tools to start a budding business or to make gorgeous wreaths as a hobby.

Nancy says: "I am thrilled to know these ladies are leaving with confidence and knowledge to set up online and offline businesses to sell their beautiful creations. But, most importantly, I am also filled with JOY as they leave with hugs, laughter, and lots of smiles."

Nancy has been encouraged, and coached by her mentor and dear friend, Jim Cockrum. Nancy admires Jim and calls him one of the most ethical Internet Marketers around, and all the while Jim says *"Nancy has inspired me more than I could ever inspire her."* As a matter of fact, Jim has written about Nancy in his newly published book; **"FREE Marketing 101"**. This book is **the number one** book on Internet Marketing in the world!

Nancy is inundated with emails and calls from her faithful followers who want and need her to help them. You see, Nancy has been fighting a painful battle with Fibromyalgia and Celiac Disease after becoming severely ill at twenty-eight years of age. Thanks to her husband, Steve, amazing doctors and God's leading; she is enjoying a new life!

Plantation Charm Wreath – How to make a wreath for your door

Nancy has a heart-felt yearning to help others regain their health, & experience positive changes as she has. She desires for each of you to find joy, health, and happiness through God's leading and through your own successful business. This has turned into quite a ministry for Nancy and Steve.

INTRODUCTION

Welcome and Congratulations on your purchase of Plantation Charm Wreath Instructional Book!

Wreath making can become one of the easiest and most delightful hobbies you will ever undertake. I taught myself how to make a wreath many, many years ago during a difficult time in my life. I was struggling to feel normal while experiencing chronic pain, so wreath making became an outlet of self-expression and creativity. I first sold my wreaths at craft shows, and after finding success there, I purchased a local shop called The Straw Basket. This purchase was a highlight in my life, allowing me to develop my own style in floral design. The business grew, taking me down several avenues, which eventually led me to eBay. I didn't stop there! I now sell wreaths to faithful customers all over the world, while other parts of my business continue to grow by leaps and bounds.

For many years I have received requests from friends, customers, and new acquaintances alike wanting to learn my style in designing one-of-a-kind wreaths. Customers and friends in my hometown tell me when they visit a home or doctor's office in town; they always recognize my wreaths and my style immediately. Well, this book is geared to instruct, but most of all to help you develop your own style, which has been and will always be my goal!

I have poured hours of labor and creativity into Plantation Charm so that you can learn the basics -- each step in building (and yes, it is a building process) your own wreath. **I will be sharing with you some of my tips and secrets for making gorgeous wreaths.** I encourage you to follow along closely and then add your own creative touch.

Plantation Charm Wreath – How to make a wreath for your door

These quality tips and secrets will help you make your very own wreath that can withstand the weather, birds looking for a place to nest, and the occasional fall from your door. If you begin each wreath or design in the right way by tightly securing each stem, bloom, bird, birdhouse, nest, etc., then your wreath will hold up for many, many years. Sun damage, which, unfortunately, is inevitable, may occur, even with quality materials.

You will also learn how to make your wreath "wild & woodsy", "light & airy", or very full and formal.

These phrases have described my personal style, but in the long run, and with lots of practice, you will eventually start to see your own style developing. This style will be exclusive to you, your likes and dislikes, and will reflect the unique and special person that you are. *I can guarantee that it will be absolutely beautiful!!*

Plantation Charm also includes a list of suggested supplies, in addition to a list of the particular items I used for the wreath on the cover. Please go to your local craft/floral store to purchase the stems that best suit your style and taste, or visit my supplies store: **www.LadybugCertified.com**. Always remember, available supplies change from year to year. You may not be able to purchase exactly what I used here. Just find something as close as you can.

I offer several books as well as instructional DVDs and digital videos and wreath design. You can learn more in the **Resource Appendix**.

Plantation Charm Wreath – How to make a wreath for your door

ITEMS YOU WILL NEED

Wreath Making Tools

- **Glue gun and glue sticks***
- **Wire cutters***
- **Floral tape**
- **Picks**
- **Pipe Cleaners**
- **Easel (optional)***

  ***NOTE:** I use a custom made easel which you can purchase here as well as other wreath making supplies: http://ladybugwreaths.com/doorwreaths/product/wreath-making-supplies/

Supplies for the Plantation Charm Wreath

(Supplies can be found at LadybugCertified.com, or your Local Craft Store or Wholesale Supplier)

- **Wild birch wreath***
- **Section of honeysuckle vine**
- **Three Large Magnolia Blossoms**
- **Two Gerber Daisies or Similar Flower**
- **Purple Pansies**
- **Lemon Spray, Grapes, Eggplant, Banana, Peach**
- **Green leafy stems such as Ficus**
- **Green grasses in several sizes**
- **Ivy bunch**
- **Two ribbons – five yards of each**
- **Freshly harvested honeysuckle**
- **Two orchid stems**
- **Lots of forsythia**
- **Moss (green)**
- **One Bird with Nest**
- **Ladybug, Bumblebee or Grasshopper (or other critters)**

MAKING YOUR WREATH

CHAPTER 1 – LET'S MAKE A WREATH

The wreath I used is one of our custom-made wild birch wreaths. A young mother, who lives in the hills of Kentucky, makes them exclusively for Ladybug Wreaths and personally drives 9 hours each way to bring them to me.

These wreaths are custom made and will be available for purchase through our new Amazon store: www.LadybugCertified.com Also, all wreaths that I design for you are made from my Wild Birch wreaths.

Plantation Charm Wreath – How to make a wreath for your door

CHAPTER 2 – WILD HONEYSUCKLE

Place the wreath on your easel or door until it hangs evenly to find a top and a bottom. You'll know when you find the right spot. I want the wild birch stems to point up, and down. This makes it look more like an oval wreath before you even begin.

If you would like to create a more "wild and woodsy" look, cut off "curly" stems from your honeysuckle vine and glue them into the outside of the wreath. The sticks along with honeysuckle vine radiating and curling out will give your wreath a look just like mine.

Plantation Charm Wreath – How to make a wreath for your door

Let's put a wreath hanger on the back of our wreath before we do anything else. Begin by picking up one of your pipe cleaners. Work from the back of the wreath, tying the pipe cleaner to one of the heavier portions of your wreath exactly on the top.

Making sure you attach it to one of the thicker, sturdier stems in the wreath assures that no matter how much weight you add, you know that your wreath will always hang securely even when a door may open and close many times during the day. We don't want it to fall off the door now do we?

Tie the chenille stem and leave yourself a loop at the top to hang it from a door hanger or a nail.

In the previous picture, you can see the loop that I made with my pipe cleaner. I make sure to secure it really well, and as you can see, it is tied to one of the thicker stems in your wreath.

If you are using a wreath – door hanger, you may not even need a loop like this, but I always add them.

Plantation Charm Wreath – How to make a wreath for your door

The wreath you see on our cover and at the end of this book is the wreath that was designed to be the "star" of this wreath course. Its base is a "wild birch wreath" which I use exclusively as the base of every wreath I design.

Plantation Charm Wreath – How to make a wreath for your door

CHAPTER 3 – INSERTING WILD HONEYSUCKLE

Have you searched for your wild honeysuckle yet? It grows wild in trees, on the side of the road, in the woods, etc. It is easy to find if you look for it and will add such a natural feel to your wreath! Make sure you look around in the springtime when it is in full bloom with its beautiful yellow blossoms. Then, remember where you saw it so you can go back and harvest it anytime you may need it. Finding the colorful, yellow blooms makes it very easy for you to spot it from the side of the road or in the woods behind your home, etc.

When you're ready to harvest some, take some garden clippers with you and cut it at the bottom. It is usually growing up the tree, so all you have to do is start pulling it down. Now, you might have to take someone with you with a little strength. We have been able to pull a lot of ours down ourselves. Be careful! One day, I pulled too hard, and ended up on my bottom on the side of the road! Ha Ha

I personally like the white look of some of the stems rather that the dark stems. The white just seem to stand out more against my birch wreaths and the variation really looks great. I don't just use the fatter stems, but use the smaller ones, sometimes clumped together, also.

Next take the fresh honeysuckle that you picked to make the wild loops and curls in your wreath. I add anywhere from 2 to 8 feet in each wreath, depending on how it looks.

The loops and curls add so much depth and wildness to a wreath – sort of like a three-dimensional look.

Plantation Charm Wreath – How to make a wreath for your door

Adding honeysuckle is so much fun, and so easy! Before any of the honeysuckle is cut, insert one end into your wreath and out the back about ½ to 1 inch.

Sometimes, it wants to curl in its own direction rather than the way I might want it to go – so I let it. It comes out natural and interesting every single time.

At this point you can cut off the excess from the back of your wreath. Secure it to a branch using one half of a pipe cleaner. Apply hot glue to your stem on the front and back just to make sure it doesn't slip out.

Plantation Charm Wreath – How to make a wreath for your door

Remember, do not cut your honeysuckle, but instead work with the long piece. You'll find fresh honeysuckle works in small and large wreaths alike.

Continue to move around your wreath, bending and twisting the honeysuckle. In the following photo, I am creating a small loop on the bottom of my wreath from a curve in the honeysuckle vine.

Secure it where the vine naturally bends back towards the wreath. Use pipe cleaners and hot glue to keep the vine in place.

Plantation Charm Wreath – How to make a wreath for your door

We don't want it to be perfectly symmetrical, so please don't try to make each side the same with loops opposite each other. All of your loops and curls need to be random. Remember, you can never add too much, so be generous.

Also, remember that honeysuckle is much easier to work with and to bend into these tight loops and curls when it is very fresh.

It will last for a while, but I like to roll it into a tight roll while fresh. Then when I use it, I already have loops which don't have to be bent again.

Plantation Charm Wreath – How to make a wreath for your door

Remember, do not cut your honeysuckle, but instead work with the long piece. You'll find fresh honeysuckle works in small and large wreaths alike.

Sun exposure or age can cause breakage in vines as they dry out, so keep yours as fresh as possible. You can then bend and twist it as you wish. I start by looping my vine out and around the bottom of my wreath.

Don't worry if the honeysuckle sticks out up to 6 to 8 inches. Depending on how large your wreath is, it will only add depth and character to your wreath. **THE WILDER, THE BETTER…I always say!**

Plantation Charm Wreath – How to make a wreath for your door

Glue pieces of moss to soften the places where you have secured the honeysuckle vine to the wreath. The moss will add more of the natural, woodsy feel that we all love. These steps may seem slow at first, but remember, we are building the foundation of a secure wreath that won't lose any of its stems!

Continue to bend and move your honeysuckle vine. You should have between 5 and 6 yards of vine, so go wild creating loops! As you can see in this picture, I am working on multiple loops that will cross over the center of my wreath.

Looking at these pictures, you can see where I added the entire length of honeysuckle vine and some moss. Don't be afraid to let it stick out too far, loop down too low, or be too wild. You can make your wreaths as wild as mine…or not. It's your choice as the designer.

Plantation Charm Wreath – How to make a wreath for your door

Using honeysuckle in a wreath is a technique that I formulated several years ago. It sets my wreaths apart from other designs giving them an extra special quality as well as giving each a three dimensional look as well as depth and texture. Ladybug Wreaths – like none other!!

Notice again how I have glued moss to multiple places in my wreath. Be generous with your moss as it only adds to the overall look of the wreath.

Look closely at the way I have done mine. But I warn you, no matter how hard you try; yours will not look exactly like this one. I wouldn't even be able to copy it. I just want you to understand the concept of letting the vine do what it does naturally!

Plantation Charm Wreath – How to make a wreath for your door

I can't overemphasize the importance of making sure each and every stem of honeysuckle is secure and tight. Give it a gentle tug after the hot glue has dried. If it is loose at all, apply more glue. Glue can be added until you get drips running out of the bottom of the wreath. That's okay; just make sure your hand it not in the way!

Pick off the glue drips after they cool and dry. I would rather have to go back and pick drips off the bottom, than have stems that might be loose and fall out!

I hope you're not feeling overwhelmed at this point in the process. I am going to walk you step-by-step in making this wreath. We're going to have a great time together!

Now that we have completed the beginning steps of creating a beautiful wreath, let's get to the exciting part – adding fruit, magnolias, and so much more! I have been using fruit in my wreaths for years now, but for many reasons, some people feel intimidated by it.

You can purchase your fruit in separate pieces, or on a garland. Just look for the best deals to save some money.

But before we jump in, here's a brief tutorial on how to use a floral pick and floral tape.

Plantation Charm Wreath – How to make a wreath for your door

CHAPTER 4 – HOW TO USE A FLORAL PICK

Using picks is very important when working with wreaths, arrangements, and more.

It needs to be secured tightly enough that it will NOT come loose. You certainly do not want picks and stems falling out of your wreath when doors are slammed, or just opened and closed a lot.

Lay the pick beside your flower or greenery stem, so that the pick extends about 1 inch below the stem. Wrap the wire down the stem with your right hand while you are twisting the stem between the fingers of your left hand... curling it the wood of the pick to bind them together.

Plantation Charm Wreath – How to make a wreath for your door

Note: It is very important in this step to wrap the wire very tightly. If you miss this step, the pick won't support your stem as you are pushing it into your wreath.

I have several FREE videos on my YouTube Channel: **http://www.youtube.com/ladybugwreaths** where you might like to really see me do this part of the process.

I think you'll enjoy all of the videos I have listed there! Do you know there have been well over ONE MILLION views on this Channel? ☺

Plantation Charm Wreath – How to make a wreath for your door

Picks come in several sizes. I always try to keep three sizes on hand at all times. A two and one-half inch pick, which is the size you see in the above pictures, is my favorite and the size most used in wreaths. A four-inch pick is good if you need just a little more length when inserting a stem into your wreath, and where you need it to extend out from the wreath a little more.

The six-inch pick is very good to have on hand. I don't really use it that often, but when I need it, nothing else will do. I always use the six-inch picks when anchoring a bird nest even if it sticks out the back when I am finished. I just cut off the excess and know that my nest will not come out. And then there are times when you have a very thick sturdy stem that needs a pick. I always use the six-inch for these mainly because it has more wire attached and I am going to need a longer piece of wire when wrapping it around both stems.

I thought you might like to see how I store my picks on my work counter. They are in a very inexpensive clear plastic container and I have them lined up by size. This makes it very easy for me to grab the size pick I need without spreading them all over my counter, adding to the mess I probably already have!

Plantation Charm Wreath – How to make a wreath for your door

CHAPTER 5 – USING FLORAL TAPE

You must always wrap florist tape on your stem after applying a pick – it keeps your wire secure and also gives that joint support.

Apply florist tape by starting at the top of the pick, and in a curling motion, bring it down the stem, wrapping the tape around itself a couple of times at the beginning and the end.

When using florist tape, keep a slight pull on it while wrapping. This stretch makes it stick to itself and stay in place. Florist tape is not typically sticky. This tape only sticks to itself, so stretching it a little makes it stick together easier. Floral tape comes in several shades of brown and green that looks natural against your birch wreath.

There is no need to wrap floral tape on a stem that does not have a pick.

Plantation Charm Wreath – How to make a wreath for your door

CHAPTER 6 – LET'S ADD LUCIOUS FRUIT

Let's get started with the grapes. Grapes are going to be the easiest fruit to put in the wreath simply because they are more pliable. I love the shape and color of these grapes. They add such a wonderful texture to a wreath.

Plantation Charm Wreath – How to make a wreath for your door

Begin by placing a floral pick on the stem of your grapes. It is important that your 6 inch pick is securely placed on the stem, so hang the grapes downward from your hand and get the pick in there. Wrap the wire tightly around the stem and the pick.

In this picture below, I am wrapping brown floral tape down the pick. Remember what I told you about using floral tape. Make sure that you pull the tape tightly so that it will stick.

Does your cluster of grapes look like mine now? As you can see, my pick is securely wrapped with floral tape, so those grapes aren't going to escape!

Plantation Charm Wreath – How to make a wreath for your door

Because a cluster of grapes is pliable, we didn't have to worry about the angle our pick was attached.

However, as you are going to find out very soon, other fruit requires you to pay careful attention to the angle of the pick for a tight fit into the wreath. But I'm jumping ahead of myself.

Plantation Charm Wreath – How to make a wreath for your door

Let's find a place for our grapes! I want them to hang down near the bottom center of the wreath. Try them in a couple of different spots before you stick the pick into the wreath.

Once your grapes are securely placed in the wreath, point the hot glue gun beside the pick and add glue. It is so important that you use lots of glue because we want our fruit to stay put.

With your grapes hanging nicely from the bottom of the wreath, let's continue by adding a fuzzy peach. Unlike the grapes, the peach does not have a stem to attach a pick to; instead, we are going to make a hole in the bottom of the fruit and insert the pick. Let's get to it!

Plantation Charm Wreath – How to make a wreath for your door

Begin by taking the sharp end of your pick and pushing it into the bottom of your peach, about an inch deep.

If your fruit is particularly hard, use a long nail and hammer instead to make the 1-inch hole.

Once the hole has been created, remove your pick and shoot hot glue into the hole being very careful to not burn yourself. In the picture below, you can see where I am adding glue to the peach. I shoot it into the hole until I see it coming out on all sides.

© 2014 www.LadybugWreaths.com, LadybugCertified.com

Plantation Charm Wreath – How to make a wreath for your door

Nest, reinsert the pick into the hole. Once it feels secure, cut off the wired end of your pick, making sure to cut at an angle.

You will see us use this process of creating a hole and securing the pick with hot glue on any fruit, just like this peach, when there is no stem.

In the following picture, you can see where I am adding this peach into a perfect spot – which is to the right and top of my grapes. Where are you going to put yours?

Plantation Charm Wreath – How to make a wreath for your door

Notice how I kept the pick long, even after removing the wired end, so that I have plenty of wiggle room to get my fuzzy peach perfectly placed.

Push the peach securely into the wreath, using a little force if necessary. We don't want this little guy to move at all!

After we've completed our wreath, we will have plenty of time to cut off any picks that stick out the back.

Plantation Charm Wreath – How to make a wreath for your door

Now, I am going to shoot some hot glue behind the peach, adding just another measure of stability to the fruit.

By placing a pinch of moss around and behind the peach (while the glue is hot), you can hide the glue and add another touch of wonderful "natural" charm.

I love using "fuzzy" peaches! They always look so real, and by adding a different texture to the different pieces of fruit, you have a great look.

You know, a big part of the art of designing is being able to use different colors, shapes, and textures together.

Plantation Charm Wreath – How to make a wreath for your door

Let's move on to our charming banana. As you are holding the fruit in your hand, you are probably wondering exactly how it is going to fit into the wreath, aren't you? Well, I'm glad you asked!

Just like our fuzzy peach, the banana requires a little more effort. But before we make any holes, take a minute to hold your banana up to the wreath and decide exactly where you want it to go.

Then, take your long pick and create a one-inch hole into the bottom of the banana. Look carefully at the picture above to see how I inserted the pick at an angle.

Plantation Charm Wreath – How to make a wreath for your door

This is the same angle that I will insert the pick into the wreath. Next, remove the pick and shoot hot glue into the hole.

After you reinsert the pick, and the glue dries, use your wire cutters to remove the wired end of the pick. Remember to cut it at an angle so that it will neatly fit easily into this wreath design.

Once your pick is securely inserted into the banana, place the it into the wreath. I am tucking mine into a spot above and to the left of my grapes. Remember to use a little force, if necessary, to make sure that your banana won't fall out of the wreath!

Plantation Charm Wreath – How to make a wreath for your door

Take your hot glue gun and generously shoot some glue around the bottom of the banana where it meets the wreath. This step ensures that you won't be losing this banana anytime soon!

Plantation Charm Wreath – How to make a wreath for your door

Once you've added the glue, tuck in a pinch of moss to cover it up. Use your hands to hold the banana in place while the glue dries.

Just remember to always be careful around that hot substance! My fingers have been "gotten" countless times!

If you do drip hot glue on your fingers or hand… PLEASE do not try to rub or pull it off. I can guarantee the skin will come with it. Go quickly to the sink and hold it under cold water. It may take a while, but eventually the glue will peel off without taking your skin!

CHAPTER 7 – MAGNIFICENT MAGNOLIAS

One of my favorite flowers, white magnolias, makes a beautiful statement in any wreath!

I have searched long and hard for the perfect magnolia stems, trying all different types of silks and fabrics. All were disappointing and droopy.

In order to have life-like magnolia blossoms, I like to use magnolia stems made from latex. These petals have a slight powdery feel. As you are out shopping for materials, you will find many different magnolia blossoms to choose from. But, many new materials are coming out all the time, so just keep your eyes open for pretty ones.

Plantation Charm Wreath – How to make a wreath for your door

Now, let's get on to the next step! Take one of your magnolia blossoms and carefully push it into the lower front of the wreath.

Because the stem is so long, it is not necessary to use a pick. We will cut the back off later.

Oh, how pretty! After you've placed your stem, shoot glue behind it, careful to stay out of the way of falling glue!

It is important that you work on a surface that can hold up to glue drips and debris. Those drips will cover your shoes if you aren't paying attention! Trust me, I know from experience!

Plantation Charm Wreath – How to make a wreath for your door

Take your fingers and carefully run them along each petal, opening up the blossom to create a lovely, natural shape. This step is especially important to do, if your blossoms were closed in their original packaging.

CHAPTER 8 – MUST HAVE REAL-LOOKING LEMONS

Before we continue with our magnolia blossoms, I'd like to make a quick detour to our sunshiny, yellow lemons. Aren't they just lovely?

When shopping for supplies, I purchased two sprays of lemons, instead of 6 individual pieces of fruit. The deep green leaves and curly-queues make these cheerful lemons even more delightful.

Instead of cutting apart the stems, let's work with the entire spray! Begin by cutting off a part of the long stem at an angle. Carefully tuck the spray into the wreath, just like I have done in the next picture.

Plantation Charm Wreath – How to make a wreath for your door

Next, carefully bend the spray into a similar shape as your wreath. The spray needs to have a circular shape that will flow with the rest of your arrangement.

It certainly would look silly for the lemons to stand straight up!

I have always loved using bright "lemony" yellow in my wreaths… and using the actual lemons is even better. You may find many different types and styles of lemons – they are coming out with more and more beautiful ones out of different materials all of the time!

Plantation Charm Wreath – How to make a wreath for your door

Once you've got your lemons in place, take one of the curly-queues at the top of the spray and wrap it around a branch in the wreath, securing it tightly.

If your lemon stem does not have this, then you can use a piece of taped wire which you can purchase on a roll.

If necessary, you can do this in a couple different places just to make sure the spray stays in place. Then, shoot some hot glue into the original place where you put your stem. Add another pinch of moss to cover up the glue.

Plantation Charm Wreath – How to make a wreath for your door

I hope that you are proud of all that we've accomplished so far! This wreath is well on its way to becoming a beautiful, charming wreath!

Now back to those Magnolia Blossoms! I am itching to add more of these beautiful magnolia blossoms to the same side as the first one.

I will balance these two out by adding a third blossom near the top of the opposite side as you can see in the following picture.

Plantation Charm Wreath – How to make a wreath for your door

Once your magnolia blossom is in the place you want it to be, shoot some glue behind it, adding moss to cover any drips.

I'm sure you're noticing how much glue and moss I am using. You can NEVER use too much. This hides all of your work (or construction) of your wreath, making it look much more professional with a finished look that many, many wreaths just do not have!

Remember keep running your fingers along the petals of the flower so that they open up in a natural way.

Plantation Charm Wreath – How to make a wreath for your door

Before we get to the third magnolia blossom, I want to take a second to make sure that all of the stems and pieces of fruit are anchored into the branches of the wreath.

I think this particular spot needs another shot of glue. Do you see any places in your wreath that might need a little extra glue? Turn the wreath around to the back and look for any unsecured places.

I found some in mine, so I am shooting it in with my glue gun… and guess what I'll do next? You got it! Cover that hot glue with more moss.

Plantation Charm Wreath – How to make a wreath for your door

Now we're ready to get that third blossom in place!

This magnolia blossom will look perfect on the upper left side. It will balance out the two that are located at the bottom. I'll show you a picture of all three in just a minute! I do want to say here that I do NOT go by the "odd or even" rule when adding flowers. I just put them where I think they look the best – whether it is 2, 3, or 4.

As with the other two magnolia blossoms, push the stem into the wreath, making sure that it is securely between the branches. Use hot glue and a pinch of moss to secure it even more.

© 2014 www.LadybugWreaths.com, LadybugCertified.com pg. 50

Plantation Charm Wreath – How to make a wreath for your door

These are large flowers, so don't be afraid to use lots of glue. You can always cover up the drips with extra moss.

Once in place, again run your fingers along the length of each petal so that they curl towards heaven!

Ta-Da! Here is our wreath up to this point! I know we still have several steps to go, but I am so proud of all that we've accomplished. We are well on our way to achieving "Magnolia Charm!"

Plantation Charm Wreath – How to make a wreath for your door

CHAPTER 9 – GREENS MAKES SUCH A DIFFERENCE

Greenery is a wonderful tool to turn any arrangement or wreath into something spectacular. For this wreath I've chosen to add Ficus stems among other greenery. Let's get started with these stems!

NOTE: I used to use Wisteria, but have switched to Ficus, and like using it much more!

Plantation Charm Wreath – How to make a wreath for your door

Begin by cutting your large wisteria stem into several pieces. I usually end up with 6 stems, or if I want them much larger, I cut it into three (I rarely do this, though). Look at the picture below, and let me show you what to do.

We will have to add picks to each piece because the stems aren't sturdy enough to push into the wreath. So, go ahead and cut your Ficus into pieces and I'll wait until you're done to show you the next step!

Plantation Charm Wreath – How to make a wreath for your door

Place the pick against the leafy stem and wrap the wire tightly around the two. The picture below shows you what it should look like.

Notice that I put the pick about an inch from the stem's bottom and then wound them very tightly together with the wire so they won't be loose and floppy or come apart.

Next, take floral tape and wrap it around the pick. Remember to pull on the floral tape so that it will be sticky. (When pulling on floral tape, it actually sticks to itself). Now, run your glue gun down the length of your stem, evenly coating it – I do it once or twice, at least.

Plantation Charm Wreath – How to make a wreath for your door

Now, let's get this stem into place!

Plantation Charm Wreath – How to make a wreath for your door

I like the way this particular piece of wisteria is angled. I think it will go perfectly near the top of my wreath. When placing greenery, make sure you notice how it "moves".

The placement should make sense and be pleasing to the eye. Feel free to try – pulling your stem in and out before securing it with the hot glue.

Now, I want to place the next piece of wisteria flowing out the wreath below the fruit.

Don't get distracted by the flowers or ribbon behind me. My shop is full of colorful baskets of stems and other design materials, so they might show up in a few photos!

Plantation Charm Wreath – How to make a wreath for your door

Remember to run your glue gun down the length of the pick before inserting it into the wreath. If necessary, add additional glue once the piece is in place!

We have a lot of greens to add, so let's keep going! Behind the two magnolias leaves is another perfect place to add leafy greens.

Notice how it is not directly opposite of the greens we just placed below the fruit. Instead, this stem is a little higher.

Plantation Charm Wreath – How to make a wreath for your door

Continue filling in your wreath with pieces of Ficus. Be sure to place picks on each stem and wrap them with floral tape.

Plantation Charm Wreath – How to make a wreath for your door

With all of our wisteria leaves now secured into the wreath, let's move on to our beautiful, green grasses! These grasses have wonderful color and texture! Be sure to buy grasses that look interesting and real.

Behind the third magnolia blossom and around the fruit are some great places to add more greens!

These stems were in one big bunch, so I cut them apart.

Plantation Charm Wreath – How to make a wreath for your door

Here, let me show you in the picture below!

Flatten your large bunch of grasses into individual stems. Use your wire cutters to cut them, making sure that you leave enough room on each stem to secure a pick. Once separated, take each stem of grass and apply your pick.

Use the same methods we used on the Ficus leaves, carefully add the wired pick, wrapping it around tightly. Once the pick is in place, wrap floral tape around the stem. Why don't you go ahead and do this procedure with all of your grasses so that they will be ready to place in the wreath?

Plantation Charm Wreath – How to make a wreath for your door

This grass goes nicely here, doesn't it? By placing the grass behind our two magnolia leaves, we've created height that emphasizes a place of interest. It draws the eye to our flowers and fruit.

In this picture you can see two stems of grass that I've placed into the wreath. In the background, notice the grass angled near our third magnolia blossom.

Just like the stem I'm placing next to the fruit, the grass flows out from the wreath to draw the eye. It also gives your wreath that loose and airy look that Ladybug Wreaths is known for. You know…our "wild & airy" look! ☺

Continue adding your stems of grass throughout the wreath.

Plantation Charm Wreath – How to make a wreath for your door

The next type of greenery we are going to add is ivy. Ivy adds a wonderful, natural feel to any wreath.

I have a wonderful bunch of ivy that I love to use, and we are happy to sell it to you. You can find it here: www.LadybugCertified.com .

As you can see in the picture above, I have separated individual stems of ivy from one large bunch and placed picks on them. Why don't you stop right now and take the time to cut your bunch of ivy into individual stems.

Plantation Charm Wreath – How to make a wreath for your door

Now, let's add the ivy to our wreath! Begin by carefully applying hot glue to the first stem.

We are going to place the ivy throughout our wreath in order to fill in some empty places.

The first ivy stem that I am placing into the wreath is going behind my two magnolia leaves. We have already put some wisteria and grass in this area, so the ivy will add a nice contrast.

Plantation Charm Wreath – How to make a wreath for your door

Be sure to push the stem down into the wreath so that it is secure. The further you can stick it into your wreath (at an angle, so it isn't sticking straight out the back), the more secure your stems will be anchored into the wreath.

Once the glue is dry, wiggle the ivy around to see it you need to add any more glue. If the ivy feels loose, shoot some hot glue into the wreath around the stem.

Plantation Charm Wreath – How to make a wreath for your door

In the next picture, I am placing a longer piece of ivy on the top of the wreath. This stem goes perfectly right here, don't you think?

Here is where I would like for you to begin using your own creativity to determine where each piece of ivy should go. Let them hang in different directions to create an interesting visual effect. Curl each stem a little. If you'll notice when looking at living ivy, it curls in many directions. Finish adding the rest of your ivy.

Plantation Charm Wreath – How to make a wreath for your door

Let's take a moment to step back and admire our wreath so far! I think we're doing a very good job!

I love all of the greenery we added. The varying shades and textures liven up the wreath and enhance the fruit and flowers.

I hope that you are feeling proud of all that you've accomplished! Wreath-making is such a wonderful skill to learn and a fun hobby to embark on!

I'm so glad that you decide to join me!

© 2014 www.LadybugWreaths.com, LadybugCertified.com pg. 67

Plantation Charm Wreath – How to make a wreath for your door

Here are two closer views of my wreath so far. Yours does not have to look exactly like mine, but it should have a similar feel to it. Don't all these colors look great together? Don't ever be afraid of color, or a mixture of colors. Each one really enhances the other.

Plantation Charm Wreath – How to make a wreath for your door

CHAPTER 10 – GOTTA HAVE A SWEET BIRD NEST

I love the special touch of charm that a bird's nest adds to a wreath. I remember as a child finding nests during springtime nestled in the crevices of the blooming dogwoods in our backyard.

I would carefully stand on my tiptoes eager to catch a peek of the speckled eggs inside. Wonder and excitement filled my innocent heart as I waited for the eggs to hatch. Ponder how you felt as a child during springtime as we start on this next step of our wreath.

Plantation Charm Wreath – How to make a wreath for your door

The first step in adding a bird's nest is to decide where you are going to place it in the wreath. Once that is decided, push a pick into the nest at an angle. Take the nest back out and apply glue over the bottom. Reinsert the nest, pushing the pick all the way into the birch wreath.

When pushing the pick through the nest and into the wreath, sometimes you may run into one of the large wreath stems. Just rotate and slide it around a little to see if you can get it to slide in. It usually slides in pretty easily after a little experimenting.

Plantation Charm Wreath – How to make a wreath for your door

Now, add a second pick to secure the nest into the wreath.

Insert this pick at the opposite angle so that the two picks cross each other. Using your hot glue, add moss to cover the inside of the bird's nest. The moss will make a cozy home for the bird that we will add later.

Both picks going at different angles really add strength so it will stay in place. Apply hot glue and a little moss around the nest so that it is secure on all sides.

Plantation Charm Wreath – How to make a wreath for your door

Once the nest is in place, use your wire cutters to clip off the top and bottom of the pick (or picks).

Once the glue is dry, use your wire cutters to snip off the wired end of your picks that are sticking out of the nest. If your nest does not feel secure add more glue underneath.

Have you noticed how we are really taking our time making sure that each element is VERY secure? I just cannot stress how important these steps are to your finished design!

Plantation Charm Wreath – How to make a wreath for your door

If for some reason, the nest still doesn't feel secure, add more hot glue as needed. Feel free to add a little moss in the nest and trailing out the front side. Make it look like the Mama bird built the nest herself!

If you see some of the picks, and pipe cleaners showing through, this would be a great time to cover them up with moss.

Just get a long narrow piece of moss, cover it with a little glue, and wrap it around the stem where the pipe cleaners are located. Make sure you add some behind also because that can show from the side.

CHAPTER 11 – FINAL TOUCHES

It's time to continue adding the special features of this wonderful wreath. A crimson orchid is just one of those wonderful things! Cut off each stem from your bunch as you can see me doing on the picture below.

Add a pick to each stem so that they will fit securely into the wreath. Don't forget to add the floral tape, as it will make your stem easier to insert.

Plantation Charm Wreath – How to make a wreath for your door

Now that your orchids are ready, let's put one behind our two magnolia blossoms.

I really LOVE the crimson red color as it pops against the green and white already in this area. Shoot some hot glue into the wreath once your pick is in place.

Our second orchid stem is going under our third magnolia blossom. It should be angled out from the wreath.

Plantation Charm Wreath – How to make a wreath for your door

If you are unsure of where to place the orchid, stick it into different spots at varying angles without adding any glue. It is much easier to remove a stem before adding any glue than after!

Once you are happy with the location, push the stem into the wreath and shoot some hot glue in. Notice how my two orchids are on opposites sides of my wreath, one higher than the other.

I also made a point of putting them in places that will draw the eye – the bird's nest and two magnolia blooms.

Plantation Charm Wreath – How to make a wreath for your door

Now it's time to add our two Gerber daisies. The addition of each floral stem makes the wreath fuller and brighter. The color of these Gerbers is especially nice in this particular wreath.

Plantation Charm Wreath – How to make a wreath for your door

Cut off a large portion of each Gerber daisy stem, leaving enough to insert into the wreath. You shouldn't need to use a pick for these flowers.

If you do have trouble fitting them in between the branches, add a pick to make it a little easier.

Place both of your Gerber daisies on the top, front of your wreath at slightly different angles. Notice how I am doing it in the following picture.

Plantation Charm Wreath – How to make a wreath for your door

Now let's get to our purple eggplant. You probably didn't expect to see this particular vegetable on your supply list, but I have a feeling you'll quickly see why I chose it.

The friendly eggplant has a beautiful color and shape that blends nicely in our wreath. It can be a bit tricky to add, so follow closely.

Begin by holding your eggplant up to your wreath to determine where it should go. I placed mine on the inside of the wreath above my two magnolia blooms.

Plantation Charm Wreath – How to make a wreath for your door

Push your pick into the bottom of your eggplant at the angle you need to insert it into the wreath. Once you've created a hole, remove the pick; shoot glue into the hole, and push the pick back in.

Remember the same steps when we added picks to our banana, and the fuzzy peach in the beginning of this book. I am doing the exact same thing here.

Plantation Charm Wreath – How to make a wreath for your door

Place the eggplant in the spot you previously found in the wreath. Shoot some hot glue behind your eggplant.

It is very important that your vegetable does not fall out of the wreath! You can see in this picture the angle that my eggplant is laying in the wreath.

Plantation Charm Wreath – How to make a wreath for your door

We've come a long way, but we're not finished yet. It's important as you are creating your beautiful wreath to step back and look at it from a distance.

Not only can you admire your work this way, but you also can see any spots that need to be filled.

Plantation Charm Wreath – How to make a wreath for your door

Rich, purple pansies are the next special features on our wreath! As you can tell in the picture below, we are definitely going to need picks on these flimsy stems! Cut off each flower leaving enough stem to place a pick on.

Because these stems are going to be short, be careful to place your pick high enough on the stem to make it secure. Wrap the wire around it tightly and secure it with floral tape. Now let's get to the fun part!

Plantation Charm Wreath – How to make a wreath for your door

My first pansy is going to nestle among the fruit. I think it looks great right here, don't you? Put hot glue on your stem before inserting it into the wreath. Once in place, you can add more hot glue, if you think it is necessary.

Our second pansy is going to stand out between a magnolia blossom and Gerber daisy. Now, that looks very pretty!

Don't push the pansy too deep into the wreath. Because it is small, compared to our other flowers, it can get lost among the foliage.

Plantation Charm Wreath – How to make a wreath for your door

Finally, I am placing a particularly pretty pansy below the cluster of grapes. The dark purple stands out nicely against the white if the magnolia.

Remember to make sure that you have enough of the stem to stick into the wreath far enough to really hold it as it catches the glue.

If not, then you should use a pick.

Plantation Charm Wreath – How to make a wreath for your door

By practicing these methods, my wreaths NEVER have anything that falls out of them.

They are made to last for years, and they really do! You'll probably get tired of your wreath and want a new color or a new style before it really needs to be replaced!

Plantation Charm Wreath – How to make a wreath for your door

The last thing we're going to be adding (for now) is our charming bird. Before our bird is ready to find his home in the nest, he needs a little tweaking.

To put it plainly, we need to cut off his legs! Our little friend won't sit securely in the nest if we leave his legs on, so grab your wire cutters and cut them off!

Once you have removed the legs, apply a generous amount of hot glue to the bottom of your bird. Be careful that you don't burn yourself as you're holding the bird.

Plantation Charm Wreath – How to make a wreath for your door

Place your bird into the nest and hold him there until the glue is dry. I just love the way our wreath is turning out, don't you?

Plantation Charm Wreath – How to make a wreath for your door

There are a couple more tiny details to take care of – adding the ladybug and bumblebee! As you know, all of the custom wreaths created by Ladybug Wreaths include our signature critters.

Very, very carefully add a drop of glue to your bumblebee. I am going to place mine on the front of my fuzzy peach. Where are you going to put your bumblebee?

Now, add a drop of glue to the bottom of your ladybug. Find a special place for her to sit.

Plantation Charm Wreath – How to make a wreath for your door

You can find all sorts of critters at your local craft store. I've added grasshoppers and dragonflies before, along with my signature ladybug. Be creative and find a critter that fits your unique personality.

Plantation Charm Wreath – How to make a wreath for your door

So, here it is – our completed wreath so far! Hang yours on a door and step back to admire your hard work. This wreath is so wonderful because we carefully constructed it, layer by layer, until it came out just beautiful! But… we're not through just yet!

Plantation Charm Wreath – How to make a wreath for your door

Our wreath looks wonderful hanging on a door, doesn't it?

© 2014 www.LadybugWreaths.com, LadybugCertified.com

Plantation Charm Wreath – How to make a wreath for your door

You could easily stop right now and proudly display this wreath for your friends and family to admire!

You did a great job and deserve the praise.

However, we aren't done yet! Continue working beside me to see how we at Ladybug Wreaths take a special wreath and then make it extra, extra special.

We're going to add a double ribbon bow, gorgeous yellow forsythia, and lots of grasses. We've never put all this extra information in one of our instructional books before, so you're in for a special treat!

Plantation Charm Wreath – How to make a wreath for your door

CHAPTER 12 – A DOUBLE BOW IS EASY

Here is a sneak peek of the wonderful ribbons, grasses, and floral stems that we're adding to our wreath! These special touches will take your wreath to a whole new level of beauty, talent, and charm.

Plantation Charm Wreath – How to make a wreath for your door

You may be wondering why there are two different types of ribbon in this photo. It's because we're going to be making a double bow! Don't be afraid of making a double bow. I promise you that you are going to have so much fun learning how to make double bows!

They add whimsy and color to a wreath, and these two ribbons are especially pretty together!

Plantation Charm Wreath – How to make a wreath for your door

Can you tell by the smile on my face that I'm excited about this double bow? A big part in the joy of making wreaths is getting to teach you how to do things you might have never learned otherwise.

Begin by placing the ribbons on top of each other and measure out thirty inches for the streamer. Pinch the ribbon between your fingers to hold that spot.

Plantation Charm Wreath – How to make a wreath for your door

Make your first loop working away from yourself. So, after pinching, pull the ribbon loop away from you, bringing it around, underneath, and back in toward you – then pinch or scrunch it together again.

Holding the ribbon in your left hand, make another loop exactly like the first one in the opposite direction going toward you this time. Once you have a "bowtie", make another loop slightly longer than your first two.

Make another loop in the opposite direction. Continue until you have four loops, resembling an "X" under the "bowtie".

© 2014 www.LadybugWreaths.com, LadybugCertified.com pg. 97

Plantation Charm Wreath – How to make a wreath for your door

It helps me to think of each step as a bowtie or X, and I hope that it will help you too! Remember that these four loops should be about an inch to an inch and a half longer than your first two loops.

Finish off the bow by making a smaller loop at the top of the bow. Do this by twisting the ribbon at the place where you are holding it, then bring it up and over to create a loop.

Twist the ribbon again so that it curls down on the left side of your bow to create your second streamer.

Plantation Charm Wreath – How to make a wreath for your door

Once you have all of your loops, use a green chenille stem, also known as a pipe cleaner, to tightly secure the bow. I can't tell you enough how important it is to make sure that your bow is tightly held together! So, don't miss that step!

Now, let's separate the ribbons to make a full bow! Hold the bow close to your body and pull each loop apart, running your fingers from the center of the loop all the way around. At the base, give each ribbon a little twist as you separate them so that they will not come back together.

Our bow looks beautiful; so let's add it to our wreath! I think it will look perfect on the front right side of the wreath.

Plantation Charm Wreath – How to make a wreath for your door

Place it near the top above the eggplant, but not directly in the middle of the wreath. Use the pipe cleaner to secure the bow to the base of the wreath. Pull the pipe cleaner all the way around a branch and to the back of the wreath, wrapping it tightly to secure it.

We don't want the streamers to simply hang down, so let's purposefully position them to fill the wreath.

You can see it better in this picture.

Plantation Charm Wreath – How to make a wreath for your door

Now, it is time to add your double bow to the wreath. It will take a little time to turn, tuck, and pull each loop of the bow exactly where I want it. Be patient, and take your time, you can do this… I know you can!

Begin by tucking one streamer behind the eggplant as you see me doing in this photo. Notice how I didn't tuck it tightly, but instead left enough ribbon to make a small loop.

Plantation Charm Wreath – How to make a wreath for your door

The streamer is still rather long; so let's make another loop with it. I do this simply by adding a pick to the ribbon.

Once your pick is in place, wrap floral tape around it to make it blend in easier. Its special touches like this that most people don't think about.

How many times have you seen wreaths with droopy bows that fall flat against the flowers? By taking the time to do these extra steps, you end up with a dynamic bow that has designer quality.

Plantation Charm Wreath – How to make a wreath for your door

With your floral tape in place, use your glue gun to run hot glue down the pick and place it into the wreath. Don't pull down on the ribbon or it will lay flat in the greenery.

Instead, make your ribbon look like it is floating gracefully in your wreath. Once in place, use your fingers to curl the mesh streamer, making nice, soft loops.

Plantation Charm Wreath – How to make a wreath for your door

Let's add one more loop with our stripped ribbon. We will do this by tying it to a greenery stem.

Tie it under the magnolia blossom so the ribbon matches the shape of the wreath. Using your fingers, add a gentle curl to the bottom of the streamer.

Plantation Charm Wreath – How to make a wreath for your door

Now, let's get to our second set of streamers. Begin by carefully pulling the striped ribbon up and under the honeysuckle towards the top of the wreath.

Leave the mesh streamer where it is, and we'll get back to it in a minute.

Plantation Charm Wreath – How to make a wreath for your door

Bring your ribbon up and around the top of the wreath and tie it around your honeysuckle vine. You don't have to make a knot, but it needs to stay in place.

I love the look of loops of ribbon curling in and around in my wreath… it gives it a totally different look. It is a look that I think you will love when you master this technique!

Plantation Charm Wreath – How to make a wreath for your door

Bring the streamer back up and around the Gerber daisies to form another loop like I have done in the picture to the left. Secure the loop near your pansy, using hot glue and moss.

If you see a hole in the branches, use a pick to tuck the ribbon into the wreath and then shoot some glue down in there. You don't want your ribbon to pop back out, so use lots of glue to make it stay in place.

Moss is wonderful at covering up glue drops.

Plantation Charm Wreath – How to make a wreath for your door

All of our streamers are in place except for the last green mesh ribbon. Instead of looping it into the wreath, I'm going to cut mine off at an angle, leaving a short end.

It will blend nicely into the greenery of the wreath. Now don't throw away that end; we're going to do something with it in the next step!

We want our wreath to look lush and full. Here's a wonderful technique that I use to give my wreaths that extra special touch.

Plantation Charm Wreath – How to make a wreath for your door

After my double or triple bow has been artfully arranged in my wreath, I use short pieces of ribbon to make extra loops and curls around my flowers and fruit. Here, let me show you how to do it!

Take the piece of mesh ribbon that you just cut off. Add a pick and wrap it in floral tape. Run your glue gun down the pick and place it in the wreath next to the bird's nest.

Plantation Charm Wreath – How to make a wreath for your door

Create a loop by tucking the ribbon under the banana. Run your fingers along the edges of the ribbon to give it shape and curl. Add a touch of glue if necessary to secure the loop.

Before we add any more loops, I want to see how we're doing so far. Let's hang our wreath on a door and step back to see how it looks. It's hard to see everything when you're working so closely.

Plantation Charm Wreath – How to make a wreath for your door

Here is my wreath so far. How does yours look?

Plantation Charm Wreath – How to make a wreath for your door

I think we should make another loop. This striped ribbon is too pretty to not add some more! Return your wreath to the easel and let's get back to work!

Measure off about 10-12 inches of ribbon and pinch it between your fingers like I'm doing here.

Bring the ribbon up and around to create a loop. Cut off the second streamer at the same length as the first one.

Plantation Charm Wreath – How to make a wreath for your door

Add a pick to the middle of the loop where you are holding it with your fingers. Wrap floral tape around the pick.

Plantation Charm Wreath – How to make a wreath for your door

Let's put this pretty loop under our grapes. Nestled in the fruit, this ribbon will enhance the natural feel from the fruit and greenery.

Push the pick all the way into the branches of the wreath.

Use your fingers to guide the streamers into soft, flowing loops. They should not hang straight down.

If you need to, shoot some hot glue behind the loop to keep it tucked into place.

Plantation Charm Wreath – How to make a wreath for your door

CHAPTER 13 – EXTRA GRASSES, GREENERY, AND TWIGS

Even though we have already added wisteria and other greens to our wreath, I think we should make it fuller with the addition of more beautiful grasses, textured greenery, and bendy twigs.

The wreath looks a little tight to me, so the addition of these flowing, airy stems will loosen it up and give it a more "wild and woodsy" look.

Begin by cutting the stems of your long grasses to separate the branches.

© 2014 www.LadybugWreaths.com, LadybugCertified.com

Plantation Charm Wreath – How to make a wreath for your door

Add a long pick and wrap it in floral tape. Go ahead and do this for all of your stems of grass. We are going to be adding fern stems along with these grasses.

Let's put some of this long, green grass in the Ficus and ivy mix.

Put some hot glue along the pick and if necessary, shoot some glue into the wreath to secure the stem. These grasses will add extra length around the wreath possibly up to 4 or 5 inches.

Plantation Charm Wreath – How to make a wreath for your door

I have a few fern leaves in my shop, so I'm going to add some of them as well to the mix.

The purpose of these greens is to add fullness and size to the wreath; if you don't have the exact same stems as I am using, don't worry about it. Use what you have and I'm sure that it will look pretty!

Before we continue with our special touches, I want to tell you about an exciting event taking place at Ladybug Wreaths. You can find them at www.LadybugCertified.com

Plantation Charm Wreath – How to make a wreath for your door

We are thrilled to now offer wild birch wreaths to our customers. These exclusive wreaths are created especially for our business and are not available anywhere else.

Because I think they are so special, I want you to be able to use them in your special creations!

I cut off these stems from the wreath when I first got started because they were simply too long. But now that I've cut them, I can add the stems back to the wreath at the heights and places I like.

© 2014 www.LadybugWreaths.com, LadybugCertified.com pg. 118

Plantation Charm Wreath – How to make a wreath for your door

I always trim the airy stems that are too long from the sides f the wreath because they can get in the way of opening your door.

Let's add some more airy grasses! This bunch looks nice here, don't you think?

It adds the height that I'm looking for and flows with the shape of the wreath.

Plantation Charm Wreath – How to make a wreath for your door

You may need to take the wreath off of your easel to get the hot glue into the right places.

These grasses are going along the outer rim of the wreath adding to the base of greens.

Plantation Charm Wreath – How to make a wreath for your door

The wreath is very full at this point, so you may need to use a little force when putting these stems into it.

Plantation Charm Wreath – How to make a wreath for your door

I found some extra Ficus leaves that I didn't use earlier, so I am going to add that into my bow. The green stands out among the pretty pinks.

I want you to see just how much extra greenery I added to this wreath, so here are several more photos for you to follow along.

How about a stem of grass right here? Remember to use a pick if necessary to get the stem into place.

Plantation Charm Wreath – How to make a wreath for your door

This bunch draws the eye to our sweet bird perched in his nest.

Plantation Charm Wreath – How to make a wreath for your door

Use these greens to highlight the wonderful flowers in our wreath. Here, this stem of grass will draw attention to our Gerber daisies. The greens sort of frame the flowers with the rich green color, just as you would find it in nature.

Airy grasses are another type of greenery I like to use. And we use grasses in every single wreath that we make – yes… even our very special Christmas Wreaths!

Plantation Charm Wreath – How to make a wreath for your door

I really LOVE the look of mixed greens, lots of color, a double bow, and all the other materials you see in this sweet picture above!

Don't you?

Plantation Charm Wreath – How to make a wreath for your door

I think this magnolia blossom needs a little more green behind it. Use your creative and talented eye to place greenery around your wreath. The added height around the entire wreath will add so much to the final look.

Here's a side shot of our wreath so far! Oh, I'm so excited to see how it is turning out!

Aren't you glad that we decided to do a "part 2" on this wreath? While it was certainly pretty before, this fuller, designer wreath is just breathtaking!

© 2014 www.LadybugWreaths.com, LadybugCertified.com

Plantation Charm Wreath – How to make a wreath for your door

The addition of our double bow, extra loops, and lots and lots of greenery are a major part of what makes Ladybug Wreaths so special. I'm so happy to be able to share these secrets and tips with you.

Plantation Charm Wreath – How to make a wreath for your door

Before we work on the last step, let's clean up the back of our wreath. By adding all of the greenery and grasses, there are lots of picks poking out of the back!

Turn your wreath around, and using your wire cutters remove any sticks or stems that prohibit your wreath from lying flat against the door.

The final touch to finish this amazing wreath is the addition of yellow forsythia. This pop of color will liven up our wreath and give it the perfect touch. You see, it's the little details that all come together to make your professional wreath outstanding!

Plantation Charm Wreath – How to make a wreath for your door

I have now decided to add some forsythia (or 'breath of spring'), as my grandmother used to call it. Using wire cutters cut off the stems at the joints, allowing for differing stem lengths.

For the shorter stems, add a pick, then wrap in floral tape to make them go into the wreath easier. The longer stems should be fine without a pick.

Now, let's put some right about here. Because this particular forsythia stem is long, it will add to the height at the top of the wreath, along with our airy grasses and birch stems.

Plantation Charm Wreath – How to make a wreath for your door

If you are unsure of where to put your stem, place it in the wreath before adding glue. Once the perfect spot is found, simply remove the stem, add hot glue and reinsert it.

The right side of the wreath is another wonderful place to add a stem of forsythia. Again, use a longer stem so that it will "flow" with the movement of the wreath.

This wreath is so full and airy. You've really done a great job!

Plantation Charm Wreath – How to make a wreath for your door

Place another long forsythia stem in the middle of your two magnolia blossoms. It should drape down the wreath, cascading forward. That yellow sure looks pretty against the white flowers, don't you think!

Plantation Charm Wreath – How to make a wreath for your door

Above the magnolia blossom on the left side of your wreath is another perfect place to add some yellow flowers.

This time, let's put the stem down into the wreath so that it stands up in the foliage and doesn't fall forward.

Plantation Charm Wreath – How to make a wreath for your door

We really want to highlight our feathered friend, so let's drape another piece of forsythia near our bird. This stem should cascade down the wreath.

Use your fingers to give it shape if the stem is lying too flat.

Plantation Charm Wreath – How to make a wreath for your door

I like the way this looks right here. Continue adding your forsythia stems throughout the wreath. Look for places that the yellow stems will add pops of color.

Plantation Charm Wreath – How to make a wreath for your door

I know I said that we were finished, but I want to add just a couple more special details. When I'm making a wreath for a client, I know that it's the little touches that make my wreaths so special. I want you to see something new every time you look at a wreath made by Ladybug Wreaths.

I found this sprig of blueberries lying around my shop; you might not notice it at first glance, but it adds something special.

Use your creativity to make your wreath unique and interesting. Again, this attention to detail is what makes your wreath so wonderful and professional.

© 2014 www.LadybugWreaths.com, LadybugCertified.com

Plantation Charm Wreath – How to make a wreath for your door

If you have any greens left over, take a minute to see if they belong anywhere. I think I just found a place!

I've decided to not add the purple flowers I pulled out at the end. I think the wreath looks perfect just the way it is!

Plantation Charm Wreath – How to make a wreath for your door

Take a moment to admire your beautiful creation, and hang your finished wreath on the front door, take in the beauty, and do a happy dance because you have just made a professional and gorgeous wreath!

You can give this wreath away, sell it to an eager customer, or simply savor the good feeling you get every time you see your hard work!

Plantation Charm Wreath – How to make a wreath for your door

CONGRATULATIONS!!!!!!

Plantation Charm Wreath – How to make a wreath for your door

CHAPTER 14 – FINISHED WREATH

Plantation Charm Wreath – How to make a wreath for your door

APPENDIX- RESOURCE PAGE

LADYBUG NEWSLETTER

Nancy's **FREE** weekly newsletter contains: decorating ideas; design tips; free 'how to' videos; or special deals. To begin receiving Nancy's newsletter, go to her website: http://www.LadybugWreaths.com . **Nancy would LOVE to add you to her mailing list!**

INSTRUCTIONAL DVDS & DIGITAL VIDEOS

Nancy offers MANY instructional videos that show you step by step how to make a particular style of wreath or bow. To view the list of video offerings, go to:

http://ladybugwreaths.com/doorwreaths/product/dvds/
http://ladybugwreaths.com/doorwreaths/download-videos/

WORKSHOPS:

Nancy offers both private and group workshops in her studio in South Carolina. In these workshops you receive personal instruction from Nancy and her assistant on the art of wreath making. You leave with the most beautiful wreath you created and with the knowledge how to make more!

Learn more here:
http://passionintoprofits.com/workshops/

COACHING:

Nancy, along with her friend and partner, Linda Joseph, offer private and group coaching. Our goal is to show you step by step how to sell your wreaths and/or other creations online.

Getting Started Coaching

Many ladies want help turning their creations into a business. "Best of Nancy" is our introductory coaching club. It consists of a forum, video training, monthly updates and bonuses. The forum is a great place to ask questions, meet other like-minded people and find encouragement. The video training covers all the essential elements for selling your creations on the Internet.
To learn more go to:
www.BestofNancy.com

We also offer extended workshops:
www.PassionIntoProfits.com/workshop2/

Purchase My Favorite Supplies From Ladybug Wreaths

Another Ladybug Wreath's site, **www.LadybugCertified.com** provides the exact same supplies Nancy uses in all her wreaths. Available from Amazon, shipping is FREE with Amazon Prime. Benefits are…no Sales Tax ID is required; no case quantities; no minimums; and super-fast shipping.

PURCHASE CUSTOM WREATHS

Nancy continues to create beautiful wreaths that are a treasure for any home. To see her wreaths currently for sale go here:
http://ladybugwreaths.com/doorwreaths/wreaths-for-sale-2/

To order a custom wreath, go here:
http://ladybugwreaths.com/doorwreaths/custom-door-wreaths/

Plantation Charm Wreath – How to make a wreath for your door

CONNECT WITH NANCY ON FACEBOOK

https://www.facebook.com/nancyladybugwreaths

SUMMARY

How to Make a Gorgeous Wreath

- Reports- http://passionintoprofits.com/free-reports/
- Workshops - http://passionintoprofits.com/workshop1/
- Physical DVDs – http://LadybugCertified.com
- Digital Videos - http://ladybugwreaths.com/doorwreaths/download-videos/

Where to Find the Best Supplies

- Wreath Supplies – http://LadybugCertified.com
- Secret Vendor List – http://MySecretVendors.com

How to Sell Online

- Reports- http://passionintoprofits.com/free-reports/
- Passion Into Profits Coaching – http://PassionIntoProfits.com
    - Best of Nancy Membership – http://BestofNancy.com
    - Workshops - http://passionintoprofits.com/workshop2/

APPENDIX - GETTING STARTED MAKING WREATHS

THREE EASY STEPS TO MAKE YOUR FIRST GORGEOUS WREATH

1. Get Step by Step Instructions
2. Buy Supplies
3. Make a Wreath

Plantation Charm Wreath – How to make a wreath for your door

STEP 1 - GET STEP BY STEP INSTRUCTIONS

I have produced well over 50 step by step instructional video tutorials and have written several instructional e-Books! The feedback I have received has been overwhelming! Here is just one testimonial:

> *"Nancy, I have just viewed my copy of your video about the two-foot Christmas tree, and I cannot tell you how much I treasured every moment of it!!! I received it a couple of days ago but put it aside until I had time to savor every minute of it like I was eating a luscious box of chocolates! I love your color choices, and not only did your tree have a wonderful burst of elegant color and glitter, but hanging the greens made the tree have movement as well. You REALLY are a Master Designer and I could watch your video all day.*
>
> *I shared your website with a professional wedding, floral designer. She was thrilled with your website and had as much of a hard time dragging herself away from it as I did!*
>
> *Thank you SO much for pursuing your heart's work through your adversities because it is a real inspiration to so many of us too!"*
> *Blessings! ~Carmela~*

[NOTE: I have hundreds of testimonials. If you'd like to read a few more, click here. http://ladybugwreaths.com/doorwreaths/how-to-make-wreaths-testimonials/]

You have just purchased the Sunflower Garden e-Book to learn how to make a wreath. How much easier do you think it would be to "watch" me while I do it and explain what I am doing? Yes, it would help a whole lot!

© 2014 www.LadybugWreaths.com, LadybugCertified.com

Plantation Charm Wreath – How to make a wreath for your door

You have two ways to learn from me:

1. Watch one of my many instructional videos

2. Let me teach you in person in my studio!

INSTRUCTIONAL VIDEO

Rather than give you a list of my DVD's to choose from, I want to make this very easy!

To get started:
Just purchase 2 DVDs: "Summer Daze" and "Ribbons and Bows" [http://ladybugwreaths.com/doorwreaths/product/dvds/dvd-summer-daze/ and http://ladybugwreaths.com/doorwreaths/product/dvds/how-to-make-a-bow-for-wreaths/]

   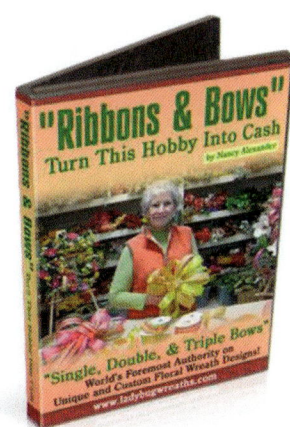

Summer Daze   **Ribbons & Bows**

All you have to do is watch these two videos! You'll be surprised at how much you learn!

Plantation Charm Wreath – How to make a wreath for your door

LEARN FROM ME (NANCY) IN PERSON!

Have you ever just wanted to have Nancy stand by your side and show you step by step how to make a wreath?

Well, now you can attend a workshop in her studio!

- **Spend the day with Nancy**
- **Learn in person from Nancy**
- **Immediate feedback from Nancy**

That's right! You can come to my personal shop and learn directly from me! We will start the day at 9:00am in my shop. You will work on your own wreath as I and my assistant lead in the design of a gorgeous wreath.

I provide all the supplies and tools and even an easel. You will be able to ask me any question you want and I will give you immediate feedback on your work. You will complete a 24 inch wreath.

You will learn to ship by boxing and shipping your wreath to your home. You finish the workshop around 4pm with a completed wreath and all the tools, as well as the bonuses.

Learn more about my workshops!
[http://passionintoprofits.com/workshop1/]

Plantation Charm Wreath – How to make a wreath for your door

STEP 2 – BUY SUPPLIES

You will need some basic supplies for making wreaths.

These wreath making materials include:

- "Wild Birch" wreaths in several sizes made exclusively for LadybugWreaths
- Wreath making easel designed by and made exclusively for LadybugWreaths
- Rolls of freshly harvested honeysuckle vine
- Klein Wire Cutters, my personal favorite
- Sure-bonder Glue Gun or any other hot glue gun

The above is a picture of some of the supplies you will need to get started. You will also need a wreath form (birch or grapevine), honeysuckle vine, and an easel (optional).

© 2014 www.LadybugWreaths.com, LadybugCertified.com

Plantation Charm Wreath – How to make a wreath for your door

WREATH SUPPLIES

I am so excited to announce that due to an overwhelming demand, we have started to provide my favorite supplies for making wreaths.

These are not just any supplies you can buy at the local craft store.
No Ma'am!
These are the supplies that I, Nancy Alexander, use in my high end wreaths!

Our store will grow, but here are just a few of the items that you will find at:

LadybugCertified.com

STEP 3 – MAKE A WREATH

First I recommend that you spend some time practicing your bow-making skills. Make them over and over again! That is the best way to learn. You can even use the same ribbon, and iron it if necessary in-between bows. The more you practice, the prettier your bows will be.

I would watch "Ribbons & Bows" over several times as you practice your bows. Please don't be discouraged if your first one doesn't turn out as you would like. But after several tries, you'll actually begin to see in your mind where each loop and streamer should be. That's the way it was for me. I did have a hard time with my first several bows.

Then, one day, something just clicked in my mind, and I thought: "WOW, I've Got It!! I can really see the bows as I am making the loops!" And, I did have it! I have been making beautiful bows ever since. And, my bow-making skills are still growing and changing to this day – as I'm sure yours will too.

I PROMISE THAT YOU CAN DO THIS!
I GUARANTEE YOU CAN DO THIS!

Next, you can start working on your wreath. Watch the wreath-making video once all the way through so you can become familiar with the terms, as well as my techniques, tips, and methods. Then you are ready to work along with my video.

Pause the video whenever you need me to stop so you can catch up. Rewind it when necessary. This IS NOT hard. It is SO enjoyable! As you get started, you'll be amazed at what you can accomplish with the correct instructions! Remember again… I know you can do it!

NOTE: Short-cut the process by working with me in person!
[http://passionintoprofits.com/workshop1/]

APPENDIX – HOW TO DECORATE A WREATH

STEP 1 - GET STEP BY STEP INSTRUCTIONS

STEP 2 – BUY SUPPLIES

STEP 3 – MAKE A WREATH

Now that you have learned how to make a wreath, you will want to start making wreaths as gifts and for special occasions. Not only will "you" want to start making more wreaths, but friends, neighbors, and even strangers will begin asking you to make wreaths for them. They will like the way your wreaths look so much, that they'll offer to hire you! This is when it is time to start expanding your wreath-making skills; as well as getting many of the questions that begin flying through your head, answered by me.

Beautiful Wreath Made in "Plantation Charm" e-Book

Plantation Charm Wreath – How to make a wreath for your door

STEP 1 - GET STEP BY STEP INSTRUCTIONS

I have many videos to choose from which cover all seasons and different occasions. Some of these videos come in DVDs, and some are downloadable. More and more are being produced all of the time. These videos include wreath making, table arrangements, table Christmas trees, and tying beautiful bows.

(You can find my DVD selection here: LadybugCertified.com/store)
(You can find my Digital Video selection here:
http://ladybugwreaths.com/doorwreaths/download-videos/)

If you aren't sure which to choose next, then I would recommend trying "Welcome to My Garden"
[http://ladybugwreaths.com/doorwreaths/product/dvds/how-to-make-a-wreath-welcomegarden/]
or "Merry Christmas"
[http://ladybugwreaths.com/doorwreaths/product/dvds/christmas-door-wreath/]
depending on which season you want to focus on, and which style "strikes your fancy".

Plantation Charm Wreath – How to make a wreath for your door

STEP 2 – BUY SUPPLIES & MATERIALS

You should have the basic supplies for making wreaths. (If not, you can review the list and purchase here.) [http://ladybugwreaths.com/doorwreaths/product/wreath-making-supplies/]

You will definitely want to look over the supplies I use in my wreaths. Go to:
LadybugCertified.com to purchase the quality supplies that I use in my Ladybug Wreaths!

Here is where I do recommend watching the video all the way through at least one time (or more). Some of the wreath-making videos have bows, and some do not – just like some people like bows in their wreaths and some do not. So, decide if you need to purchase ribbon.

When I am purchasing supplies, I usually pick out my ribbon last. It will be much easier to match it to your flowers this way (or at least until you are a little more experienced).

You should buy your materials based on what you see me use in the video you are viewing.

First, you'll notice that I use a large mix of greens.

Plantation Charm Wreath – How to make a wreath for your door

As you can see in the pictures above, I show you a large mix of greens as I discuss the many types and colors that look great in a wreath! And, I really like using at least three different types of greenery or more such as:

- Short grasses for tight or accent spots on the inside of your wreath. These are great to tuck in and around birds, nests, birdhouses, etc.
- Longer grasses which I use mostly from the outside of the wreath giving it a larger, wilder, and airier look.
- Ivy – I prefer mini leaf with long streamers so it can drape out from the wreath as well as wrapping around some of the honeysuckle vine and wild birch sticks radiating from your wreath.
- Then I always use leafy stems such as wisteria or ficus – and there are many more types of leafy stems. You can get GREAT prices on these if you have purchased "My Secret Vendor List". You can read about it here: "My Secret Vendors". [MySecretVendors.com]
- OR -- You can order the supplies I use here: **LadybugCertified.com**

Plantation Charm Wreath – How to make a wreath for your door

The pictures above are clips from a video where I show you which flowers I am using. Take note of the types, sizes, and colors of flowers and berries used in the video you have purchased.

- If I am using two or three large flowers, then it will be easier for you to follow along with me if you have two or three large flowers.
- The same applies if I am using medium and small size flowers. Try to purchase stems as close to what I am using as you can. Choose colors that you would like to use.
- Pay special attention to see if I am using a flat flower like a Gerber daisy or a thicker, rounded flower like a hydrangea or a mum. Even this will make a difference when making a wreath for the first time. Later, you'll be able to make substitutions easily.
- And, I also use spiky flowers around the outside of my wreath to bring color out from the center. You can find these in many sizes and colors. Some are called Delphiniums, and then others may just be called flower spikes.
- If using fruit, pick out fruit which you would like to see in your wreath, and the same applies for stems of berries such as crab-apples, or just tiny berry stems.

Plantation Charm Wreath – How to make a wreath for your door

STEP 3 – MAKE A WREATH

Now you can start making the wreath while you watch the video. Pause the video when you need me to slow down!

ALTERNATIVE – ATTEND A WORKSHOP

I have been asked countless times if I would teach in person. And, I have coached many women as time and health permitted through the years, but not nearly as much or as often as my customers have wanted. So, I will now begin running workshops in my home studio.

We will be offering a limited number of one-day intensive with just "you" and "me". My time will be your time for an entire day! I will teach you how to make any type of wreath that your heart desires!

© 2014 www.LadybugWreaths.com, LadybugCertified.com

Plantation Charm Wreath – How to make a wreath for your door

Next, will be the one-day, Intensive small group workshop. There will be four or five ladies just like yourself. My assistant, Kim, and I will work one-on-one with each of you as we demonstrate how to make a beautiful wreath. You'll be making yours right along beside us!

Thirdly, is our Premium Intensive TWO day workshop which includes making a wreath as well as learning important business practices, Facebook Page setup, Etsy store setup. You will go home with a beautiful wreath for yourself or we can list it on Etsy, ready to sell! This workshop is designed to REALLY take your wreath-making skills as well as your business to the next level.

Each of these different coaching sessions include, your very own wreath supplies (wire cutters, glue gun, pipe cleaners, picks, floral tape, and green sheet moss), a custom designed "Ladybug Wreaths" easel and a beautiful, finished wreath.

If you are interested please fill out an application at:
http://passionintoprofits.com/workshop1/

APPENDIX – HOW TO SELL YOUR WREATHS

Now that you have learned how to make different types of wreaths and have gotten positive feedback from family or friends, you may want to start making some money from your hobby.

Nancy started out years ago selling on eBay and had tremendous success there! It was a great start to her business. However over the years sales started slowing and she looked for other places to sell online.

After a lot of research, Nancy found that Etsy was the best place to sell your wreaths.

NOTE: If you have spent any time on the Internet, you have seen a lot of changes in the Internet and you need to shift your marketing strategies to maximize your online sales.

Etsy has become such a popular venue for handmade items (as well as vintage and other items) that is it not easy to get found and have a lot of sales.

The first step is to start selling on Etsy. You will want to set up your store and list several of your items. Next you need to send interested buyer to your store.

Next we recommend that you create a Facebook page and start building a list of fans who like your creations. This does take time but is a great way to get started.

After you have your Etsy store and a Facebook page, you will want to setup a Pinterest presence. This is a great place to interact with others and to build a following. You can create boards for your different creations.

How to sell online:

Plantation Charm Wreath – How to make a wreath for your door

1. Etsy (your store)
2. Facebook (your audience)
3. Pinterest (exposure and audience)

BONUS – JUMPSTART YOUR BUSINESS

There is nothing like taking the 'fast track' to starting a business online. I made so many mistakes when I first got started but I plowed through the difficulties even though it took a lot of time and money. However, my income soared once I hired a coach--someone who took me by the hand and guided me through the pitfalls and eliminated my 'trial and errors.'

You can research and figure out how to do this over time. However, there is nothing like taking the 'fast track' to starting a business online. We made so many mistakes when we first got started but we plowed through the difficulties. Even though it took a lot of time and money, we have been able to make a great income.

However, our income soared once we hired a coach--someone who took us by the hand and guided us through the pitfalls and eliminated many 'trial and errors.' Although we are both hard and determined workers, never again will we waste time by trying to build our business without the guidance of a coach or mentor.

We offer two ways to 'jumpstart' your business:

1. Community/Training
2. Workshops

Plantation Charm Wreath – How to make a wreath for your door

COMMUNITY/TRAINING

[Best of Nancy Community](http://BestofNancy.com) (http://BestofNancy.com) – The purpose of this community is to have a place for members to interact and ask question as well as provide the training needed to start selling online.

There are two major benefits to being a part of this awesome group:

- Forum - The favorite place to hang out for all the members is the forum.
    - You get to know each other and share successes
    - You can share difficulties and get advice and encouragement.
    - You can ask questions when you are stuck

    There are several sections in the forum:
    - Etsy – Member stores and how to use Etsy
    - Facebook – Member pages and how to use Facebook
    - Pinterest – Member Boards and how to use Pinterest
    - YouTube / Websites / Business Strategy/Planning
    - Making Wreaths
    - Boxing Wreaths
    - Shipping Wreaths
    - Website
    - Videos/Checklists/PDFs/Audios
    - Much, much more
- Training – Video instructions on how to sell on the Internet using:
    - Etsy
    - Facebook
    - Pinterest

Plantation Charm Wreath – How to make a wreath for your door

- Website
- Videos/Checklists/PDFs/Audios
- Much, much more

Plantation Charm Wreath – How to make a wreath for your door

WORKSHOPS

(http://passionintoprofits.com/workshop2/)

Our Premium Intensive TWO day workshop enables you to improve your wreath making skills as well as setup your business!

- Day 1 – Nancy will work with you to take your wreath making skills to the next level! You will leave this portion of the training with a beautiful wreath!

  You have all of Nancy's supplies to choose from and you will receive your own wreath making supplies: wire cutters, glue gun, pipe cleaners, picks, floral tape, and green sheet moss.

- Day 2 – Focus on starting your business. We will set up your Etsy store and show you how to create your first listing which will be one of the wreaths you just made in Nancy's shop. Nancy shows you how to take pictures.

  We will then setup you Facebook page and link your Etsy store to your Facebook page. You will learn about business practices, the best way to use social media to build your business and your next steps.

  Your business is started when you leave!

Printed in Great Britain
by Amazon